TONE BERGLI JONER

THE DOUGH BOOK

NORTH LIGHT BOOKS
Cincinnati Ohio

CONTENTS

First published in North America, 1991

North Light Books
an imprint of F&W Publications
1507 Dana Avenue
Cincinnati Ohio 45207

ISBN 0-89134-405-5

Printed and bound by Times Publishing Group, Singapore.

FOREWORD

Making dough figures is fun for all the family and it soon becomes quite addictive. It is an opportunity for everyone to gather round the kitchen table — children and parents, relatives and friends. The kitchen is the centre of the action. All the raw materials needed are there in the cupboard: flour, salt and water. The dough is lovely to knead, easy to shape and dries well in the oven. With water-based hobby paints available in a range of exciting colours, it is amazing what you can conjure up. Making dough figures is a fascinating hobby for the whole year round.

The best thing about making dough figures is that each generation can share the fun of making something together. It is a pursuit that is suitable for pre-school and school children, grown-ups and the elderly. In Scandinavian youth clubs the boys are just as keen and enthusiastic as the girls, and old-people's homes organise courses.

In the beginning people sometimes worry about making a mistake, but it does not take many evenings to become really skilful and find out how much fun it is. Most people start with something simple — so as not to be discouraged. You can find everything you need at hobby shops, apart from the dough itself.

You will find modelling ideas in all kinds of places: at home, in books, in nature, and hopefully, in this book. There are more than 150 ideas certain to inspire both young and old. Eighteen artists have contributed their ideas. Their initials are shown after the captions and their full names are on page 11.

Pre-school children have a creative imagination and are capable of producing results far beyond what we might expect from such young people. However, it is really a hobby for everyone. It is just a question of getting started.

Good luck!

The Dough

This is a good recipe that is just right for baking a tray of small figures.

2 level cups (8oz/225g) of wheat flour
1 heaped cup (4oz/100g) of common household salt
¾ cup (6fl oz/150ml) of lukewarm water
1 tbsp wallpaper paste
1 tbsp oil

Some people think wallpaper paste and oil are unnecessary, and that the dough is good enough with just flour, salt and water. Others think the paste makes it easier to join the various parts together, and that the oil makes the dough more supple. However, if there is no oil or paste at home, do not let that hold you back. With this dough, it does not matter if you leave out those two ingredients.

I think it is a good, firm dough, one that does not crack as easily as others I have tried out. But if you are not happy with it, you will find alternative recipes on page 10.

It makes no difference whether you measure with a cup, mug or glass, but it is easier to obtain an exact ¾ measure if the container has straight rather than curved sides.

Blend together the flour and salt — and if necessary the paste-powder — and pour on the water and oil. It is fine to use cooking oil or sunflower oil, but some people think olive oil or peanut oil increases durability.

Stir well in the bowl and pour the mixture out on the table (oilcloth makes a good base).

The dough looks crumbly and dry, but when you have kneaded it steadily for about 10-15 minutes you will have a dough that is both supple and firm. With such a consistency, the figures keep their shape better; they are less likely to collapse, or get blisters during baking. It is better to knead it a little longer than to add more water too early.

You can test the dough by holding a roll straight down for about half a minute. If it keeps its shape fairly well, the dough is good; if it quickly pulls itself down a great deal, then it is too wet. In that case put a little flour on your hands and knead it in.

On the other hand, if the dough is too dry, even after a large amount of kneading, mix in an extra teaspoon of oil, or just moisten your hands.

When kneading you may find it easier to divide the dough into two parts and knead one lump at a time.

Once the dough is just right, it should be left for 30-60 minutes, well packed in plastic or a container with a tight-fitting lid. The most important thing is not to let any air get in, as this will dry out the dough.

It does not matter if the dough is left for a few hours, or overnight, since it can be kept cool for a few days. But take it out an hour before you intend to use it. If kept for a long time the dough may get too damp; you then have to knead in a little flour and / or bake it at a low oven temperature. However, for the best results, use newly-made dough.

What you do

It makes sense to start with something simple. For example, you could use an egg cup to press out a little door-plate. Roll out the dough to a thickness of about 1cm(⅓in) (you do not need to use flour). Even though the front side of the dough may have a few cracks, the reverse side can be smooth and even, so turn it several times.

You can also press out figures using gingerbread cutters, or make Christmas decorations and jewellery. One possible idea is to roll two balls and attach them to make a little troll. After baking stick on fur or wool to simulate hair.

It is not difficult to make a simple little garland by just twisting two dough rolls. If you want to feature candles, then before baking make the holes for them using a candle. You can also decorate the garland with flowers and leaves by flattening out five balls as garland leaves round a dough ball. Put the smallest leaf in the middle, let the others overlap each other, and you make a rose; draw one end to a point and you have a leaf. (See *Individual Parts*, pages 12-16.)

Hanging

It is easiest to make a hole or loop for hanging while you're shaping the dough. Use a thick straw for making holes since it takes away excess dough and does not distort the shape. (NB: make the hole at least 1cm($\frac{1}{3}$in) from the outer edge, as otherwise it will not hold.)

You can also squeeze a paper-clip in from the top (gold is best, since it does not rust); alternatively, place it just below the back edge by pressing a piece of dough over the lower part of the paper-clip. Bend out the upper part slightly from the figure. This helps in two ways:

1) The paper clip does not show.
2) There is a small passage of air between the figure and the wall, and it continues to dry.

Other possibilities include twined loops of brass, copper or florist's wire, all available in hobby shops. Extra strength may be gained by bending up the "legs" on them. But make sure you press thoroughly round the spot where the hanging part (the hook) sits. (See *Individual Parts*, pages 12-16.)

Tools

A spatula is handy for shaping and patterning, but a table knife is equally effective.

An ordinary garlic crusher (not one with loose parts) makes the finest "spaghetti-hair", sheep's wool, treetops and grass. Failing that try using a colander or a tea-strainer, but I have to say that I prefer a garlic crusher!

Toothpicks are useful for strengthening the bond between the head and body on a figure, but they are not essential. A match or paper-clip serves the same purpose. Toothpicks are also good for drawing and imprinting patterns, as are all kinds of household things: nozzles, thimbles, funnel spouts, coins, forks, corks, buttons, combs, straws, boxes, pieces of lace and lots more. Use your imagination!

Remember to clean all metal tools after use; otherwise they can blacken or go rusty owing to the salt in the dough.

NB: the golden rule when fastening parts of the body and individual details is to use water as "glue", so have a small bowl of water ready nearby and a paint brush with which to apply it. (Remember that in days gone by people used to make glue out of flour and water.) Water also helps to smooth out any cracks on the figure before baking.

Colouring the dough

It is fine to knead colouring agents such as cocoa, coffee powder, paprika, curry powder and cinnamon into the dough. Juices from beetroot, carrot, fruits or spinach may be mixed in the water before kneading the dough. Do remember, though, that coloured dough should not be baked at a temperature greater than 125°C(280°F).

However, most of the items described in this book are painted after baking.

The base
Shape the figures directly on to the baking paper on the baking tray or on a loose piece of baking paper. Then use a spatula to move them to the baking tray, shifting large items with a strong piece of cardboard underneath. In that way you avoid the "hammock effect", which can distort the figure's shape.

Baking and drying

Most ways of baking dough are variations of three principal methods:

1) *Long drying*. You dry the figures at a temperature of 75–80°C(180–190°F) for about 12 hours, or at 50°C(130°F) with fan-assisted ovens. Small items are usually thoroughly dry by this time, though larger articles can usefully be turned and dried for another day/night. This method uses up a great deal of energy, but many people think it is the gentlest and safest way of stopping the dough from rising or cracking.

2) *Gradual increase in temperature*. You start with a cold oven of 75–90°C(180–210°F) and bake at this temperature for 1–2 hours; then 1–2 hours at 100°C(230°F), 1–2 hours at 125°C(280°F) and so on until the figure is done at around 150°C(330°F). At high temperatures it is important to check carefully that the figures do not get burnt, rise or crack.

3) *Rapid baking*. Some people think small figures should be baked for two to three hours at 110–120°C(250–270°F).

The reason for the different methods is that ovens vary so much, and there are also differing opinions on whether or not fan-assisted ovens are so efficient. But if you don't have much heat coming from below, speed up the process by placing the baking tray right down in the oven.

The Vienna bread effect
The higher the temperature the more easily the dough rises, which leads to the Vienna bread effect: air bubbles in the figure. In this condition it becomes fragile and can easily crack or later break into pieces.

If you spot the dough rising in the oven, take it out immediately, prick it with a needle in several places, carefully press out the air, lower the temperature and continue baking. Pricking the thickest parts with a needle both before and during baking is a good way to avoid bubbles.

High temperatures create a brown colouring and so should only be used if you are pushed for time or do not wish to paint the figure afterwards. Painting with milk increases the burnt effect. If you are intending to paint, method 1 (long drying) is just as effective, since it results in a white colour.

Variations on the theme
Opinions differ on whether or not the oven door should be ajar during the baking process. Some people start baking with a slightly open door, and after a while shut it completely; others keep it closed the whole time. Then there are those who use fan-assisted ovens and insist that it is unnecessary to have the door open.

All agree, however, that you must cover the tray with baking paper or aluminium foil to avoid rust, and many people bake several trays at a time. If you're worried about the figures getting burnt you can always cover them over, and also use aluminium foil as a means of support.

Oven grids allow a free flow of air from underneath, and after a couple of hours it is a good idea to transfer the figures to one, hard sides down. NB: the soft side will mould itself round the oven grid, and soft dough easily assumes the shape of the base. That is why the grid has to be completely level, without any grooves.

As long as the temperature rises no higher than 50°C(130°F) it is perfectly all right to bake figures complete with dried flowers, herbs or spices stuck in them.

When is it done?
You can test it two ways:

1) Tap lightly with your finger on the back of the figure. The sound should be "hollow" and even all over; if it is faint and dull anywhere the figure is not ready.
2) Try to push a needle through the figure: when finished this should not be possible, and the surface will be as hard as stone.

If you want to stop baking for a while, you can do so after a couple of hours. Later on put the tray in a cold oven and let it slowly heat up again.

Sun-drying
In the summer why not dry dough in the sun? A gradual warming is best, transferring the figure from the shade to the sun if it is really hot. It will be done in three to seven days. It is worth giving it an extra bake in the oven afterwards for an hour or two at 100–125°C(230–280°F).

Bring in the figures if the weather turns humid, since the salt in the dough attracts moisture. If the figure has softened it can be oven-heated until it is hard again.

If you want to economise you can also air-dry the figures indoors over a few days, and harden them off afterwards in the oven for a couple of hours. Choose a warm place for the operation, eg on a heated bathroom floor or on a rail over the radiator (but not on a stove because of the fire risk).

Painting

You can paint with watercolours or use markers. Top coats are best with watercolours, but a number of pleasing effects may be achieved by letting watercolours flow over into each other.

If you want a brightly coloured effect, use white as a base, or apply several coats of paint.

When using watercolours, finish off with a clear varnish (see *Varnishing*, page 8), but before doing so wait at least a day until the figure is completely dry again. Watercolours make for lots of moisture!

When you are making dough with children, it is advisable to use watercolours, but leave the varnishing to the adults because of the solvent in the varnish.

Solvent-based hobby paint
This is also known as enamel paint. It is available in fairly small tins and it gives a fine, glossy finish.

The drawbacks are that it takes six hours to dry, contains solvent, and after use the brushes have to be washed in white spirit. So it is not suitable for children, and adults must make sure they clean everything thoroughly after using these paints.

Water-based hobby paint (Acrylic)
In recent years this new, simpler-to-use paint has been appearing in most hobby shops, and in a number of stationers. It is non-toxic, odourless and contains no solvent; brushes may be cleaned in water, and the paint is completely dry after 15–45 minutes. It is excellent for decorative patterns: for example, after five minutes you can paint patterns with flowers on a plain surface.

But be careful: once the paint is dry, it is very hard to shift! So only wear clothes that you do not mind getting soiled; Dad's old shirts make ideal artist's overalls.

However, if you do spill paint on to your best clothes, soak them in water at once, and wash your hands frequently. It is a good idea to have a bowl of water and a roll of kitchen towel on the table.

You must also rinse the brushes thoroughly, but do not leave them standing in water, as that ruins them. Give yourself a good start with three different brush sizes.

Some hobby shops sell the paint in plastic bottles complete with spouts to enable you to squeeze out a little at a time, while others sell it in tubes or cans. The paint comes in a range of colours and tints, is economical to use and gives a nice finish. But you should still use varnish if you want the articles to last.

Gold and silver paint is also available and it should be used in preference to gold and silver markers which can blur or dissolve under varnish.

Colour blends

If you do not want to buy lots of paints it is possible to manage with the primary colours of yellow, blue and red, together with black and white, and various mixes of them.

A small amount of red + a large amount of yellow = orange
A small amount of blue + a large amount of yellow = green
Green + red = brown. Mostly red gives more of a grey shade.
Red + blue = violet. Mostly red makes mauve.

In my experience mauve does not come out so well if blue is mixed with pure red. It is better with blue and shocking pink. The best thing is to buy shocking pink and violet separately.

Black + white = grey
Red (shocking pink) + white = pale pink

As a general rule, we can say that you get lighter colours with white, and more subdued colours with a touch of black.

Varnishing

All dough should be varnished after painting, even if a glossy, water-based hobby paint has been used. Unless they are varnished, the figures run a greater risk of drawing in moisture, softening and eventually cracking. They are also much easier to clean when varnished. Two coats will ensure that the varnish reaches every part, but do not forget to varnish the back!

There are various types of varnishes available, both matt and gloss: some are colourless and water-based, while others are solvent-based; there are special kinds for floors, cars, and boats.

Varnish in aerosol sprays should be avoided. It is easy to use, but not environmentally friendly, as the CFC gas in many sprays contributes to the destruction of the ozone layer around the earth.

Varnishing watercolour-painted dough

Here you must use solvent-based and not water-based varnish, and this also applies to baked, unpainted dough. The reason for this is that the salt in the dough causes a chemical reaction which makes the figure crumble.

Varnishing water-based hobby paints

With such paints either water-based or solvent-based varnishes are suitable. That available in hobby shops is usually good enough. The more the figure is exposed to moisture and changes of temperature, the more coats of varnish are needed.

Floor, furniture and car varnishes give the best protection; of these, car lacquer (as it is called) is the fastest drying. Experiment, but do first try out the varnish on something that you are not frightened of ruining. That way you will avoid any disappointments. Ask at your hobby shop for advice and choose a varnish that goes with the kind of paint you are using.

Cleaning

After using solvent-based varnish, clean your hands and brushes in white spirit or turpentine.

Children and Dough

The great thing about dough is that the whole family can get involved. You can even make up a family picture together.

But make sure that children, especially the younger ones who are trying things out for the first time, get most of your attention. If you were planning to concentrate on your own "work of art" or do something a bit complicated, I should advise you to let it wait, as you will be interrupted by a thousand-and-one questions.

If you are prepared for dough-work to be dominated by the demands of the children, you will be able to share their eagerness and fun in being able to shape and paint. Remember to use water-based hobby paints that are suitable for youngsters; and if you are handling lots of kids at once, expect some riotous enthusiasm.

However they can also be very upset if things do not go well, so it is a good idea to put some gingerbread cutters on the table. Help them roll out the dough so that they can cut out a door-plate, or some stars or hearts for Christmas-tree decorations. You can also bake a few of these in advance to let them practise painting first. This always goes down well.

The most important thing is not that they make a work of art but that they experience for themselves the joy of creation.

It is always fun for children to make or give away something that adults can use, like the door-plate or Christmas decorations.

Safety

NB: not all ovens are child-proof, and when you have lots of excited children crowding round it is important to protect them from burns. Oven-door guards that afford protection from temperatures of up to 150°C(330°F) and detachable magnetic handles are available in specialised trade and department stores.

Tell the children that they are not to bake dough when they are on their own at home.

You should also decide whether or not to use paste in the dough when there are lots of children present who might stuff the dough into their mouths. Pastes made with vegetable glue generally contain harmless ingredients, but they do have a little preservative added, so children should not take in more than a tablespoon.

However, the dough usually tastes so salty the child spits it out anyway!

Air the room thoroughly during and after the use of solvent-based paint and varnish, since solvent vapours are often harmful if inhaled over a period of time.

Many varnishes are also inflammable so you must not smoke in a room where varnishing is taking place.

Keeping Dough figures

Dough figures will not tolerate moisture, so you cannot use dough to make external door-plates or decorations for a clammy bathroom. Neither do they like large temperature swings, so they should not be kept near the oven, nor in a room which is often aired.

On the other hand, you can have plates on the outside of the bathroom door or on a door inside the hallway. They are fine in the living room, especially on interior walls and in non-draughty window bays.

If you follow these guidelines, you should be able to keep your dough figures for many years.

Alternative Doughs

Many dough artists have their own particular variations of the basic recipe; a few of them are listed below.

If you are not happy with the dough described on page 4, or if you like experimenting, try one of these. If you have sensitive skin, choose a less salty dough.

Substituting potato flour for wheat flour makes dough that is good for small detailed work.

If there is too much dough, or too little, you can double, treble, or halve all the measures. Add or omit the paste or oil if you wish.

Dough 2 (quite soft)
2 cups (8oz/225g) flour
1 cup (4oz/100g) salt
1 cup (8fl oz/225ml)
  water
1tbsp oil

Dough 3
1kg (2¼lb) wheat flour
1kg (2¼lb) salt
3tbsp wallpaper paste
3tbsp oil
21fl oz (600ml/1.3pt)
  water (oil included)

Dough 4
½kg (1½lb) flour
1kg (2¼lb) salt
18fl oz (500ml/1pt)
  water (sprinkle on a
  little flour and knead)

Dough 5
½kg (1½lb) flour
125g (5oz) salt
12fl oz (350ml/¾pt)
  water
1tbsp wallpaper paste

Dough 6
2½kg (5.5lb) flour
1kg (2.2lb) salt
A good litre (2.2pt) of
  lukewarm water
6tbsp oil
6tbsp wallpaper paste

If things go wrong

Dough

DOUGH IS GRITTY: the salt has not properly dissolved, so knead further and wait. If necessary try a less salty dough (the dough described on page 4 has a low salt content).

DOUGH IS TOO DRY: it is insufficiently kneaded, or not moist enough. In this case add a teaspoon of oil, or moisten the palms of your hands and knead a little longer; then leave for a short while.

Baking

FIGURE LOSES ITS SHAPE: if the figure warps or bends during baking, you may not have made it substantial enough. This particularly applies to plates and other flat items. Next time, roll out the dough more thickly: approximately 1cm(⅓in) thickness is ideal.

DOUGH BLISTERS DURING BAKING: the temperature is too high for the dough to tolerate. Lower the temperature, remove the baking tray and read the section on baking.

DOUGH CRACKS DURING BAKING: the dough is too loose or too moist, or the temperature is too high. Lower the temperature, remove the baking tray and stick the figure together with water, or new dough plus water. You can also wait and glue after baking.

PARTS FALL OFF DURING BAKING: remove the figure and stick the parts in place again with dough and/or water. Continue baking; if necessary, glue when figure is cold.

Varnishing

VARNISH FLAKES OFF: either the figure is not quite dry or it has too high a salt content. Remove the flaky part, dry it and revarnish with the correct varnish. (See *Varnishing* on page 8.)

FORGOTTEN TO MAKE A HOLE FOR HANGING: use strong glue to stick picture hooks to the rear (a hanging arrangement with adhesion from the back). You can buy what you need from hobby shops or possibly paint or hardware stores.

After a while

FIGURE CRACKS: it may have been hanging in too moist a spot, and/or is not completely varnished on the back allowing moisture to get in. It may have been insufficiently baked, and not be fully dry. Stick the crack together with dough, paste or some other glue.

FIGURE SOFTENS OR COLLAPSES: it has been hanging in too moist a spot. Dry it in the oven at a low temperature and revarnish it completely.

FIGURE COLLAPSES OR CRUMBLES: try and stick the pieces together again with paste, joiner's glue, school glue, contact adhesive etc. If it is too much of a jigsaw puzzle, make a new figure, with a slightly better hanging arrangement this time.

Tips

If there is not much heat from below, place the baking tray right down in the oven.

Some golden paper-clips break easily when bent. Ordinary paper-clips are stronger, and you can varnish or paint them to prevent rust.

It is a good idea to stick felt pads (such as you see on chair legs) or felt patches to the back of a door-plate to protect the door and/or the plate. Also attend to any warping that may have occurred in the plate during baking. (Stick on an extra piece where the plate protrudes from the door.)

List of artists
Dough-figure artists whose work is figured in this book

R.H.P.	Reidun Hafstad Parkes.	M.E.	Monica Evensen.
A.E.H.	Anne-Elin Hansen.	S.I.J.	Sverre Indris Joner.
K.W.	Kristin Wickman.	J.W.	John Wheeler.
I.L.	Inger Leiner.	B.J.	Bente Jarevaag.
T.B.J.	Tone Bergli Joner.	H.N.	Henriette Slorer Jacobsen.
L.J.	Lisa Jacobsen.	G.S.	Grethe Syvertsen, photographer.
M.M.	Margrethe Moscoso.	L.F.	Laila Fjellberg.
E.N.	Else Nygård.	R.S.J.	Randi Schanning Jørgensen.
K.L.	Kjerstin Langebraaten.	B.P.	Brenda Porteous.

Figures

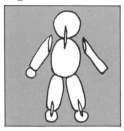  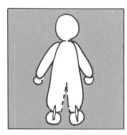  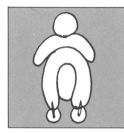

A figure made from two balls and four dough-rolls.

A woman. A toothpick joins the head and feet to the body.

Another way of doing legs is to cut or carve.

A figure with neck. The body is made from two dough-rolls.

A tubbier figure with an extra ball or oval.

Clothes

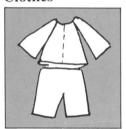    

Sweater/jacket, sleeves and trousers in four (or five) parts.

This dress has been cut or carved out of rolled dough.

Folded neatly and evenly round the body, with water to make it stick.

The dress can have raglan sleeves or ordinary sleeves.

The parts finally stuck on with water.

Hair

"Spaghetti" hair from dough pressed through a garlic crusher.

Hair in rolls: the streaks are made with a knife or fork.

Short-cut "spaghetti" hair.

"Spaghetti" hair or thin dough-rolls in plaits.

Hair made from lots of small dough-balls.

Faces

Painted eyes, nose, mouth and rosy cheeks.

Nose and cheeks made from lumps of dough.

Glasses made from wire, eyebrows and beard from "spaghetti".

Eyes, eyebrows and teeth made from lumps of dough.

Small ball for the nose, the eyes and mouth painted.

12

Hands

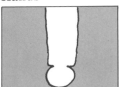

A ball.

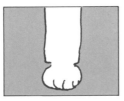

Painted "fingers" on a lump of dough.

Snipped fingers.

More clearly defined "fingers".

An arm leading into a hand with painted "fingers".

Feet

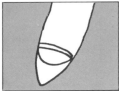

A shoe painted onto a leg.

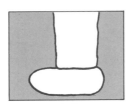

A shoe made from an oval lump of dough.

Moulded or cut from rolled dough.

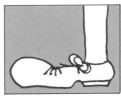

A Chaplin shoe.

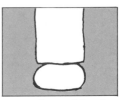

From a lump of dough.

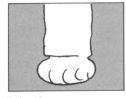

Painted toes.

Snipped toes.

Flowers

From six balls.

Five flattened balls make petals. A ball is in the middle.

Oval petals. Balls in garland formation.

"Spaghetti" with small balls.

A Swiss-roll of dough makes a rose.

Tulip cut from rolled dough.

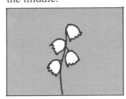

Make lily of the valley with a pastry cutter.

Baskets

Cut from rolled dough. Twined handle.

Woven from strips of rolled dough.

A basket design made with a spatula or knife.

A hollow half-ball with various objects in it.

Turn the bowl/plate upside down. Bake with smooth or woven edge all around to arrive at a hollow basket.

Leaves/fruit

A flattened ball shaped to a point.

Edges made with pastry cutter.

Cut or carved edges.

Long, thin leaves made from rolled dough.

Ball and whole clove = apple.

Bunch of grapes made from lots of balls.

Two larger balls = cherries.

Trees/grass

Carved from rolled dough, with balls as apples.

Treetop made from "spaghetti" dough.

Tree-top of large leaves.

Trunk made from dough-rolls with smaller leaves.

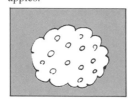

Lump of dough or cut out from rolled dough.

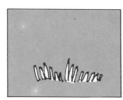

Grass made from "spaghetti" dough.

14

Text and letters

Painted on base.

Letters made from dough-rolls.

Long dough-roll.

Using twigs, matches, toothpicks.

Jewellery

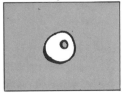
Round balls, hole with a straw.

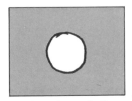
Flat brooches and clips cut from rolled dough.

Paper-clips stuck down into flat ovals.

Necklaces shaped by gingerbread cutters.

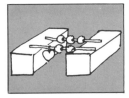
Jewellery dried on needles or sticks placed over milk cartons.

Sharpen a stick at one end: "pierce" the ball and paint it completely.

Animals

A sheep or lamb made from dough-rolls.

A dog made from "spaghetti" dough.

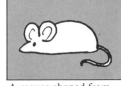
A mouse shaped from lump of dough.

A hen on eggs shaped or cut out from rolled dough.

A cat made from ball and oval lump.

A pig shaped or cut out.

Garlands

From a dough-roll.

Two dough-rolls entwined.

Three plaited dough-rolls.

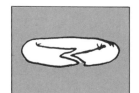

One method of joining up (use water).

Hanging

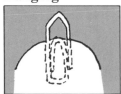

Gold-painted paper-clip stuck downwards from top.

Paper-clip on reverse side covered by a lump of dough.

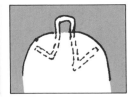

Paper-clip stuck down with "legs" bent outwards.

Entwined florist's, copper or brass wire.

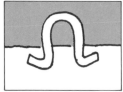

Loop.

Hole made with straw.

On the following pages Henriette (15) and Veronika (12) show how they have made six different figures.

By Lisa Jacobsen
Photos: Grethe Syvertsen

Even though some of the dough figures are made directly on the baking-tray, it is best to shape and bake them on a piece of baking paper.

The pictures show different types of paint, but for children it is best for reasons of health and practicality to use water-based hobby paints.

Remember that the dough will stay supple longer if it is kept in plastic or in a moist towel.

If your work table may stain then cover it over. The same applies to clothes.

A FESTIVE BATH SCENE

Use your imagination when you make framed pictures, as it is those little details that make them fun. Small pictures are ideal as presents since you can create on them the very features of the person to whom you are giving them.

1.

Begin with the background wall of the picture, which should be thick and firm. Then the frame, made from a roll of dough, the floor (carpet) and the bath tub can be set in place.

2.

Do the hair before putting the bath-cap in. The arm is a roll of dough lying over the edge of the bath.

3.

Here all the details have been put in place. The foam and the tassels on the slippers are dough ruffled with a fork. When you put in the details moisten the dough with a paintbrush dipped in water — they will adhere better.

4.

When you paint it is best to begin with the most prominent colour: here it is white. The flowerpot on the wall is hollow so that it can be filled with glue and dried flowers after baking.

4

1

2

3

DOOR-PLATES

Door-plates are easy to make in many different shapes. Remember the hook to hang it on, or push a hole in the plate with a thick straw.

1.
Roll out the dough to a thickness of 5mm($\frac{1}{4}$in) then punch out the plate with a glass or cup.

2.
The girl figure is made fairly flat. Use the glass to take away dough where you are going to place the plate. The arm is curved up while you press out the half-circle for the plate.

3.
Carefully press with a finger so that the plate adheres neatly to the figure. Place the arm across last of all, and attach the balls of dough which become feet under the edge of the skirt.

4.
To avoid cracks in the dough, which can occur when it has been lying too long, knead it again with a little oil. The fingers can be cut out with scissors. The plaits are made from three rolls of dough interlaced before being set in place. The plate is varnished over the dry paint.

1

2

3

4

19

SANTA CLAUS

Establish the basic form of the figure before you dress it up. You can make patterns for the clothes by placing greaseproof paper over the figure and cutting out the different parts of the garments according to the pattern.

1.
Make a small ball for the head and a larger, slightly oblong one, for the body. Then make a roll for the arms and divide it into two parts; do the legs the same way. For the jacket, roll out a little dough. Use a pair of scissors or a spatula or kitchen knife on three of the sides to make sure that the edges are even.

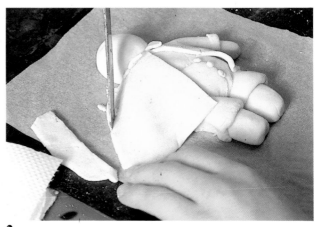

2.
Use the knife to trim away any surplus dough from the sides, and carefully press the arms firmly along the body.

3.
A cheese slice is good for raising the garment when trimming away superfluous dough. Make an incision on the inside of the sleeves and turn them up as cuffs.

4.
The fur edge round Santas Claus' jacket is a roll of dough, pricked with a toothpick. The hair and tassels are made with a garlic crusher. The shoes

are two dough-balls fastened to the legs with half a toothpick. The porridge pot with a handle made from twisted wire is empty, so that it can be filled with cotton wool or paper after baking. Small blemishes such as cracks in the face can be camouflaged with paint.

1.
When the background wall has been rolled out, the table top is modelled first, then the upper body and head. Moisten with a damp paintbrush before the arms are put in place.

GRANDMA

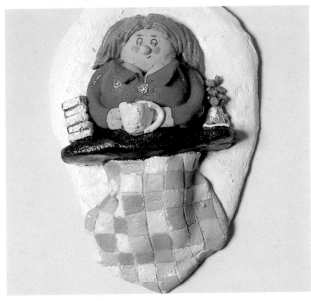

2.
Cut a nick in the dough before the dress is laid on, and fold out a collar. The pile of books has been placed on the table.

The back of the chair is not so even round the edges, but originality is more important.

If you do not have baking paper or foil moisten the baking tray with water before the dough is laid on.

21

3.

To remove the hair neatly, it is cut from the garlic crusher with scissors.

4.

If the figures feel soft when you take them out of the oven they must be baked for longer. Tap the reverse side of the figure: if you hear a hollow, even tone they are ready.

A PRINCESS

Free-standing figures need "reinforcement", made from whatever you like, other than plastic or any other material which will melt in the heat of the oven. The dough should not be too soft.

1.

Small bottles will do for reinforcement. The roll of dough is divided into two to become arms, the largest ball is the head, and the two small balls form the bosom.

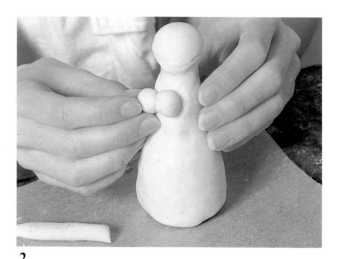

2.

The bottle is covered with rolled-out dough, which should not be too thin (4–5mm or $\frac{1}{4}$in). The head is placed on the top of the bottle and shaped smoothly into the neck.

3.
The flounces of the dress are made from thin, rolled-out dough cut in strips. Make the flounces long enough to be wrinkled and begin with the bottom.

4.
Feel free to use a screw cap if you want to mix the paint with white to obtain different shades of colour in the flounces. If you have used glass for reinforcement the figure should not be baked in a temperature above 75°C(180°F).

WINDOWS

A window can be stuck on to coloured cardboard, and you decide for yourself whether it will be a dark, starry night or a summer sky with white clouds. Here the curtains are spotted, but if you want a lace pattern on them, take a thick piece of lace and roll it on the dough.

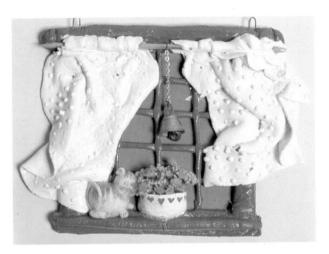

1.
The window frame and the bars are made of rolls of dough of different thicknesses. You can make room for flowerpots by shaping and flattening out the dough-roll against a knife blade held over and under the window frame.

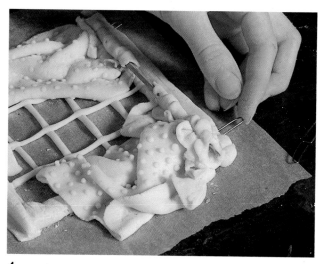

2.

Light, airy curtains should be rolled out thinly. Cut an even side edge with a knife and use a cheese slice or spatula when you transfer the curtains to the plate. A perforated ladle makes fine spots.

4.

For hanging, paper-clips are pushed into the dough before baking (*see also* picture 1). Remember that the flower pot is to be hollow so that it can be filled with glue and dried flowers after baking. A little bell hangs from the curtain-rod on an off-cut piece of chain.

3.

Wrinkle the curtains when you lay them round the curtain-rod (a thin stick of wood). The curtains look most natural if they are allowed to fall their own way, without trying to adjust them afterwards. The kitten on the window frame is placed in front of the curtains, so it is done last.

DOOR-PLATES & PLACE CARDS

1. Here are four lovely place cards pressed from rolled dough. The heads are complete with "spaghetti" hair and the extras joined on with water. If you want to use the cards for guests write their names on sticky labels (which can then be replaced). (B.P.)

2. Nordic theme showing skier and Viking ship. (S.I.J.)

Insert the brass hooks (press in hard round the holes) and make key holders out of dough. The flowers and leaves are cut out and stuck on after baking. (T.B.J.)

The sleeping child with "spaghetti" hair is resting on a cloud cut from rolled dough, roughly 1cm($\frac{1}{3}$in) thick. The stars and moon are painted on. (T.B.J.)

3. Three doors that can be used as key holders, door-plates or wall decorations. The handles are made from painted dough; for the patterns press square shapes into the dough. (T.B.J.)

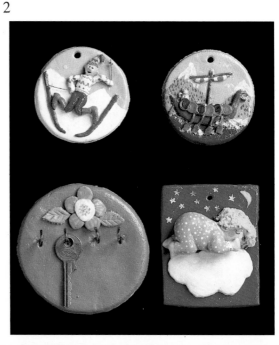

4. This cute little girl can hang wherever you like, and not just on the toilet door. It is easy to make: press the hair through a garlic crusher over the two half-balls fastened to the "night furniture". (E.N.)

5. The three round door-plates at the bottom are pressed out with a bowl from rolled dough 1 cm($\frac{1}{3}$in) thick.

The round plates for the bathroom door and WC were punched out with a glass. The motif and words are painted on with water-based hobby paint.

The holes in Adam's door-plate were made with a straw, and the lettering left unpainted. (B.P.)

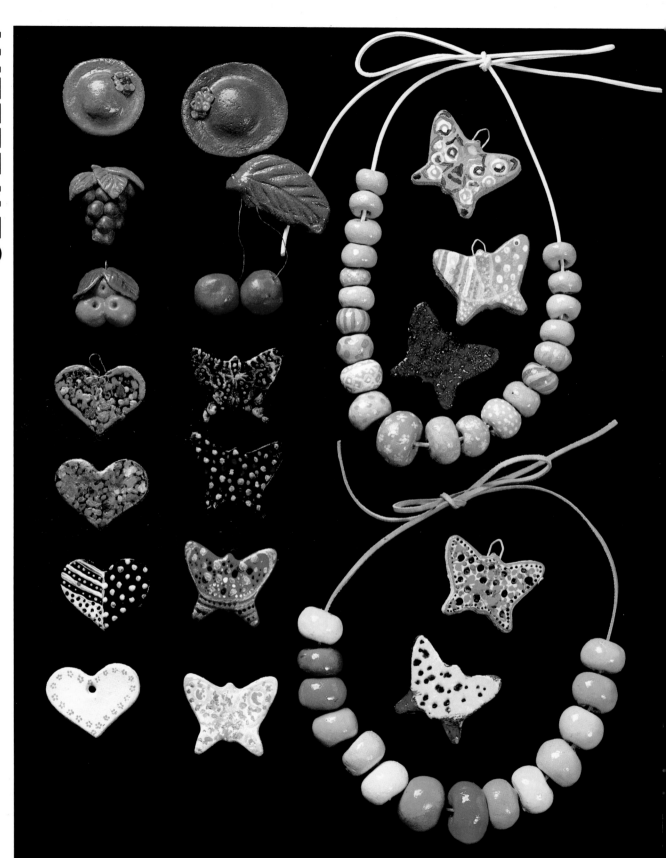

2

2. These ducks are painted with both enamel paint and water-based hobby paint. The two to the left are decorative brooches, while the duck at the bottom right has a green-painted paper-clip, and can be hung round the neck. (M.E.)

1. The decorative brooches shaped as hats consist of a circle cut out and placed on a half-ball. The crown of the hat can also be placed on top of the circle. Brooch pins are available in hobby shops, and these can be baked in, or using strong glue, stuck to the reverse side after baking. (E.N.)

The bunch of grapes consists of many small balls and an ordinary safety pin, attached to the back with glue and a plaster. All of this is painted. (E.N.)

The three apple-balls may be used as brooches, or you can also thread a leather strap through the paper-clip stuck to the reverse side. (E.N.)

The cherries are fastened with green thread to a large leaf with a pin at the back. (M.M.)

The top two hearts were painted by an eleven-year-old, and the blue-and-yellow butterfly by a six-year-old child.

The hearts and butterflies are taken out with a gingerbread measure. Holes or paper-clips are used for the necklace, or a pin glued to the reverse side.

You can punch holes in the balls using a straw. They can be painted, varnished and threaded to a leather strap or silken cord (available in hobby shops). A good way to dry them is to thread them up on needles, or the spokes of an old whisk, and hang the sticks between two milk cartons.

The more you paint the balls, the brighter and cleaner the colours will be. (T.B.J.)

1. These ball-trolls are easy to make. Just roll up two balls, and join them together with a toothpick, using a little ball for the nose. The troll is baked and then the face, skin, and clothes are painted. The hair is stuck-on fur or wool. Add various accessories, such as a necklace, scarf or tie.

The troll-girl in the middle has a tail made from dough. Before baking it is fastened on with a lump of dough but it breaks off easily. You can also make a tail from wool, or from a strip of fur with a tuft on the end. Glue it on after baking. (T.B.J.)

2. The troll-boy at far left and the troll-girl to the right complement each other's colours; and they seem to have taken a shine to each other. (K.L.)

The old man in the middle: make up two long rolls for the legs, going right up to the neck. Fix the arms on top, shape a sweater from rolled-out dough, and place it over. Then add a waistcoat and roll out some balls and shape them into feet. Cut toes and fix each foot under the trousers. A paper-clip joins the body to the head, so that it sits firm and snug. Squeeze out hair and eyebrows with the garlic press. Shape the ears and nose, and fix them with a little water; then slip a metal ring through an ear. (K.W.)

3. The troll with a little green spruce forest on his head. A good way to avoid making hands is to cut pocket holes in the trousers. (S.I.J.)

2

3

31

1. The basket at bottom left is painted dark green, while its pattern is engraved and painted yellow. On the lid there are willow twigs, chicks and white eggs. A cord is made from a thin dough-roll, placed under the lid, and around the basket. A dough-roll is shaped into a handle, and it all hangs up by a paper-clip. (R.H.P.)

The cock is painted in beautiful colours and has ostrich feathers stuck on. You can use all kinds of feathers, or make them from dough. It hangs up on strong, curved, painted wire. (K.L.)

The spring-green basket with a twisted handle also has an engraved pattern, and rests on a circular mount, extracted from rolled dough. The eggs are balls, rolled out a little more pointed at one end, and painted after baking. (The hanging hole is made with a straw.) (T.B.J.)

The chick with the red bow-tie: roll a little oblong ball for a body, then shape a wing and press it on. Roll a new ball for the head, and draw out from it a tip for the beak. The band for the bow-tie is cut from thinly rolled dough. (K.W.)

The egg with the newly hatched chick is formed from two half-balls: clip or carve out the notches. (K.W.)

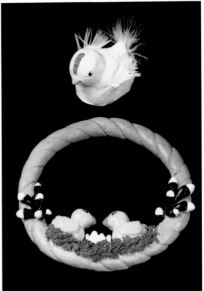

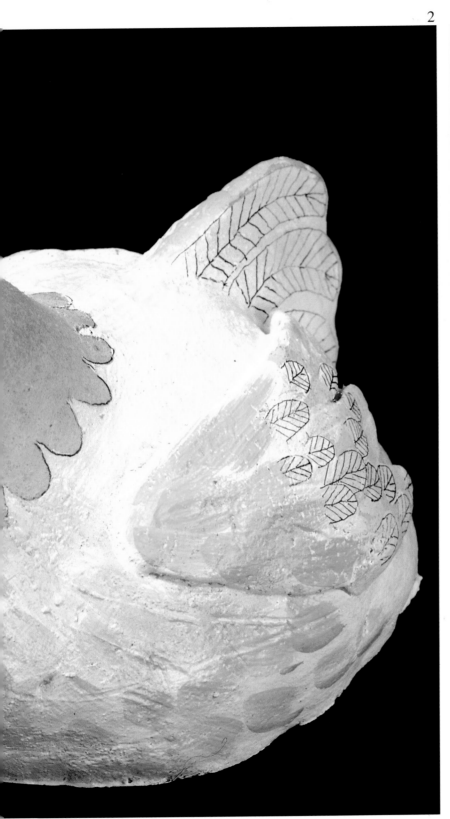

2. The splendid, stout hen is shaped over a bowl (which can withstand oven heat). Arch it with the bottom up. Oil the bowl so that it is easy to free it from the dough after baking. NB: the bowl must be well down, so that you are able to free it. (K.L.)

3. The chick at the top is shaped over an egg cup; its feathers are glued on after baking. (K.L.)

   The garland consists of two dough-rolls twisted round and joined together into a ring. The chicks are made as in picture 1, while the nest is squeezed out with the garlic press. Cut notches on a hollow half-ball for the egg-shell. Pussy willows are made from dough-balls, rolled to a pointed shape at the ends. Cut a stripe where the grey colour is to begin. (K.W.)

1

1. It is easiest to model the girl in the window straight on to the baking paper. First wrinkle the curtains, made from thinly rolled dough, then shape the window frames round the curtains. Model the girl and attach her to the bottom frame. The natural baking colour has been kept for the girl's skin, hair, and for the frame. (K.W.)

2. First cut the window from a flat piece of dough, then stick the bars and the frame on top. Finally cut out the curtains from thinly rolled dough and wrinkle; the tie-backs and pelmet are made from a flattened dough-roll.

After baking paint everything except the bars of the window. Paint the mountain background after baking. (A.E.H.)

2

34

3. Cut out the house from rolled dough; the window frames, flower boxes, and tree trunk are dough-rolls. Cut the crown of the tree from flat dough and shape it with your fingers. The apples and cats are made from dough-balls.

The ground can be cut out in one piece with the house, or laid on top. Shape it with your fingers and decorate it with pieces of grass, moss and dried flowers after baking. Then stick the straw on to the roof.

If you do not have any straw use dried grass or pine cone seeds. The chimney and house decorations are made from dough-rolls.

4

4. A Greek village measuring 25x25cm(10x10in). Roll the dough to a thickness of 1.5cm($\frac{1}{2}$in) and then cut out the background. Next, from slightly thinner dough, cut out square or rectangular shapes in various sizes and put them together as houses, balconies, steps etc. Use toothpicks for balcony rails and shape the pots round your little finger or the paint brush. Glue the dried flowers into the pots after baking; the arches and door frames are thin dough-rolls. Paint the window panes. Use two strong paper-clips for hanging. (R.H.P.)

5. A red-painted house that also looks good as a door-plate. Cut out the house from a flat piece of dough, and make the windows, door frame and eaves from flattened dough-rolls. The dough-roll that has been used for the tree trunk should be parted into two branches, and the flattened crown of the tree placed on top. Press out the grass with a garlic crusher. The flowers are made from small dough-balls pushed firmly in with a cross-tipped screwdriver. Carve the pattern on the timbers and door with a spatula or knife. (I.L.)

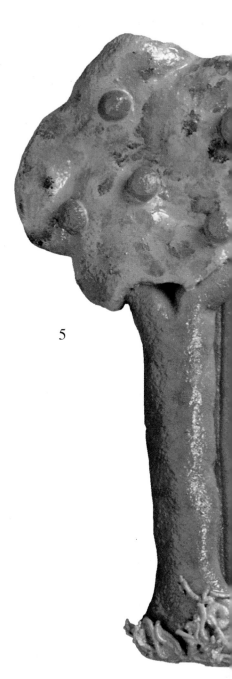

5

GARLANDS

1. A simple dough-roll: cones, artificial berries and leaves have been stuck into the dough and dried at low temperature. Do not forget to varnish the underside. Hang with a silk ribbon and decorate with silk bows.

2. The two small garlands are made from dough-rolls. The apples are whole cloves and small berries have been pushed in between the folded leaves. (M.M.)

An unpainted garland (below) made from a dough-roll. The roses have a "Swiss roll" centre and overlapping petals; the leaves are cut across the middle like coffee beans. The berries are small dough-rolls. (K.L.)

1

2

3. A garland woven from three long dough-rolls. Start weaving in the centre, otherwise one end may finish up thinner than the other. The tail of the squirrel is pressed through the garlic crusher, just like the flowers he and the little hare are holding. After baking paint everything white, then colour the animals and flowers. (M.E.)

FIGURES

1. Donald Duck and Goofy immortalised in dough. If you are inventive you will find lots of scope among cartoon characters. (S.I.J.)

2. The children, little animals and bicycles are made from balls, lumps and rolls. Use an egg cup for the bicycle wheels.

The pram is cut from a piece of flat dough, 1.5cm($\frac{1}{2}$in) thick, while the cover is from a thinner piece. Use rolls for the handle etc. (R.H.P.)

The comical long-legged pair on the sofa have rolls for legs and balls of dough for their heads and upper bodies. Use a flat piece of dough for the back of the sofa, and rolls for the seat and cushions. (Made by a five-year-old.)

3. A couple of babies with two large lumps for legs, a ball for the upper body, and two rolls for arms. One final ball makes the head, and a little tuft of "spaghetti" hair adds the finishing touch. (R.H.P.)

4. A little philosopher with big socks and shoes. Cut out the pockets. (T.B.J.)

2

3

4

41

5. A chubby little boy with a patterned woollen jumper and a girl with a pelerine collar. They have been painted with ordinary enamel paints. (E.N.)

6. Mother with two children, doll and teddy bear. The two brothers are sticking together (just for once?). The faces, legs and teddy bear are unpainted. (M.M.)

7. Three good friends from Grandma's time. The kitten is easy to make: it is one oval and one round ball, plus a roll for the tail. (M.M.)

8. Two little characters kitted out in traditional Norwegian costumes. Their skin and hair remains unpainted. (K.W.)

9. Pippi Longstocking in black-laced shoes; the laces are made with a garlic crusher. (K.W.)

10. A couple out on a trip in anoraks, knickerbockers, home-knitted socks, woollen caps and mittens — and of course, the rucksacks. (K.W.)

11

12. The lady in blue was made by an eleven-year-old. Notice how simply but deftly the face has been done.

The dapper soldier has a blunderbuss made from a stick with dough on it.

The "artist" is made from two dough-balls, as is the girl, with arms, feet and pinafore. (T.B.J.)

The little telephone has a paper-clip at the top and can be hung round the neck or kept on an "odds and ends" shelf. If you do not have a dice for your game, it is easy to make one from dough! You can even cut out some dominoes. (T.B.J.)

A ten-pin bowler deep in concentration. (I.L.)

11. The market stall and flower pots are brown-baked dough. The awning will keep its shape in the oven if you spread some aluminium foil underneath it. When you have painted everything, stick dried flowers into the pots. (K.W.)

13

13. A keen angler with a fishing rod made from a twig. The fishing line and hook are made from a piece of bent wire. You will need tools to bend the wire for the glasses. If you don't have any netting you can crochet some.

15

14. This bridal couple is "built" around two small empty bottles. Both the suit and dress are of thinly rolled dough shaped round the bottles. The heads are attached to the bottle caps and the individual details put on last; the hair is a lump of dough ruffled with a fork. After baking, stick on the lace, veil and dried flowers. NB: glass will only tolerate a

temperature of 75°C(180°F).
(R.H.P.)

15. A couple ready for folk dancing in traditional Norwegian costumes with white shirts and red waistcoats. (M.M.)

16. The striking couple on the left are all dressed in white. The lace and dried flowers have been glued on after baking. (R.H.P.)

The bride on the right is slightly more up-to-date: the dress, bouquet and brown-painted hair are sprinkled with glitter in light turquoise and pink.

The groom looks very stylish in his morning coat. (M.M.)

CLOWNS

1. The weightlifting clown is made from dough, which has been coloured using colouring powder (available in hobby shops); only the face and hands have retained their natural colour. Coloured dough must not be baked in temperatures higher than 75–90°C(180–210°F). (B.J.)

2. The red-and-white clowns are shaped from dough-rolls and their clothes are cut out from rolled dough. The hair is "garlic-pressed" and the shoelaces are also cut out from rolled dough. (K.W.)

The clown in black and white has a complete costume: the flouncy collar is two rectangles cut from thinly rolled dough, and wrinkled at the neck, while the shoe and hat ornaments, and the nose, are dough-balls. The trumpet is a long dough-roll, with a ball at the end, shaped like a trumpet-horn (actually called a bell). Everything is painted with enamel in red, black, white and gold. (K.W.)

1

2

49

SUMMER

1. The young couple are joined at the shoulders (before baking). There is a natural brown colouring on the skin, hat and hair. (K.W.)

The tree on the left and the grass are pressed through a garlic crusher. The boy is easy to make — only the head and arms are visible. (K.W.)

The girl on the far left has layers made up of petticoat, pinafore and pantalettes. The boy is in a sailor's outfit with peaked cap; his hands are hidden in the trouser pockets. (H.S.J.)

2. To do this splendid summer picture, first make the grass, which you pattern with a fork. Shape the tree using lots of dough-rolls; the apples are dough-balls painted red while the bushes are made from a flattened lump of dough, also patterned with the fork; alternatively, wind thin dough-rolls into circles. The flowers are either rounded pieces or balls; put in the lively characters at the end.

It is best to shape this one directly on to the baking paper. When you have baked and painted the whole thing, stick it on to cardboard and frame it. (J.W.)

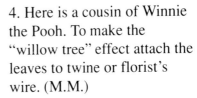

4. Here is a cousin of Winnie the Pooh. To make the "willow tree" effect attach the leaves to twine or florist's wire. (M.M.)

3. You can also work together on a scene. In this one, for example, an eleven-year-old made the birds, cats, half the tree and two of the children, and Mummy did the rest. The top of the tree was worked with the fingers. (N. and R.H.P.)

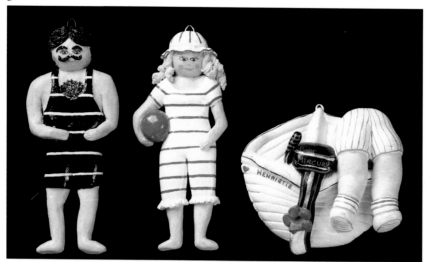

5. The bathers on the left are well kitted out for a cool summer. (K.W.)

Make the boat as follows: first take a piece of flat dough for the stem, fit the stern of the boat to this, and then the girl who is having the engine trouble. (R.S.J.)

6. The lady at the top is made from two balls that sank together into a sitting position. But with the help of a pillow and a pair of legs the figure turned out well after all. (T.B.J.)

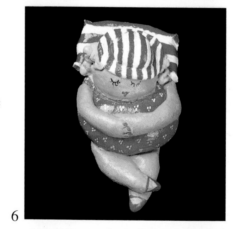

7. This mermaid reveals the fine detailing that can be achieved with dough. Note the scale-patterns on the fish tail, the rosy cheeks and bright eyes, and the golden hair. (B.P.)

8. A "jokey" band of pirates: notice the simple but decorative way of creating waves from a long dough-roll. (M.M.)

Only a real seaman can climb the rigging and finish

9. A happy concertina player: he can be hung on the wall by means of a brass wire twined round the neck. (J.W.)

his rum at the same time! (J.W.)

Some pirates come to a sticky end.

The pirate at bottom right has concentrated his efforts on finding the treasure. The chest is made from four flat pieces of dough. (J.W.)

The terror-stricken sailor on the left must have come upon the pirates Harold Fairhair and One-Eyed Jack. (H.S.J.)

1

1. An elephant and a bear, on this occasion dressed in sweaters and trousers. Made by an eleven-year-old artist.

2. The polka pig is made from three flat dough-balls: first make the body, then the head and snout. Last of all, put on the ears, legs and tail. After baking it should be painted in red and white.

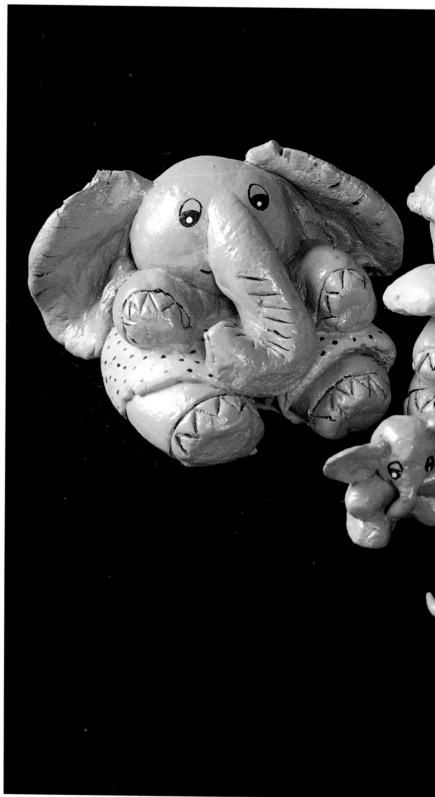

3. These elephants are all made from U-shaped dough-rolls. Skirts, trousers, forelegs and heads etc are attached to these.

4. This koala bear is made from two large flat dough-balls for the head and body, and small dough-balls for the ears, nose and feet. The arms are dough-rolls, and the hands and toes are snipped with scissors. (B.P.)

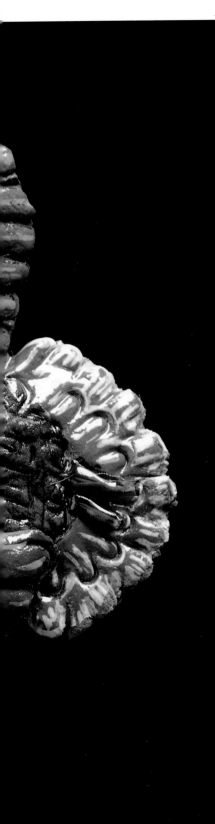

5. A naturalistic duck: the fine colours have been painted on using both solvent-based enamel paint and water-based hobby paint. It is finished off with clear varnish. (M.E.)

6. A stylised black-painted bird. The black feathers are glued to the wing, then the bird is painted. (K.L.)

FRAMED PICTURES

1. An impressive study of a lady at a coffee table: the parts are assembled, baked, painted and glued on to the background. An old black frame was used. (L.F.)

2. No one would forget a gift like this: it should be framed and hung from the living room wall. If you look closely at the picture you will see that the couple on the box of chocolates have been reproduced in dough, thus creating an effect similar to that of a portrait. (J.W.)

1

2

5. It is very easy to make the plate above, together with the spoon and fork, all from dough. Bake, paint and glue on cloth.

3. Here is a nice present to give to a musician. The instruments are baked, painted and glued to a background. (S.I.J.)

4. The bass guitar is made in two parts. Attach the neck and head, with balls for the machine heads, to the body of the guitar. The pick-up and string attachments are glued on last, then paint and varnish it. You can find small frames in hobby or photographic shops and department stores. (S.I.J.)

6. Two seasons: the subjects are shaped, baked, painted and glued on to drawing paper. In the winter scene, the roof of the house and the windows are chequered using a spatula (or knife), and the snowflakes are painted. A fork is good for the bushes, and for the fence use chopped sticks, parts of an old whisk, matches or toothpicks.

The summer apples are attached to the crown of the tree which has been ruffled up with a fork or pressed through a garlic crusher. Dough-rolls make up the tree trunk. Simple dough-balls become very pretty when they're painted into flowers. (H.S.J.)

7. A glorious apple tree, suitable for hanging. Look at the rich colours that can be achieved. (B.P.)

8

8. Two family pictures, both made with flat dough as a background and with rolls for frames.

The picture on the left has an additional picture on the spotted wall behind. To make the cat, simply use a ball for the head with a little body (or paw) peeping out. (K.L.)

The bridal couple on the right also have a decorated background. One clever thing with frames is that you can make half-length pictures. (M.M.)

9

9. Make the double bass in the same way as the bass guitar described and illustrated on page 59. (S.I.J.)

1

2

1. The wood-burning stove and shelf above are cut from rolled dough and joined with the "stove pipe". After baking and painting, glue on toothpick ladles, lace and dried flowers. (R.H.O.)

2. Roll out a large square. Cut out the bed and mattress in one piece, then carve out each mattress. Attach the bed legs, chamber pot, pillows, upper body, arm, head, hair and crown; then the cover. Draw and paint the squares later as a patchwork quilt. Finally do the curtains. Use two paper-clips for hanging, then bake everything. (K.W.)

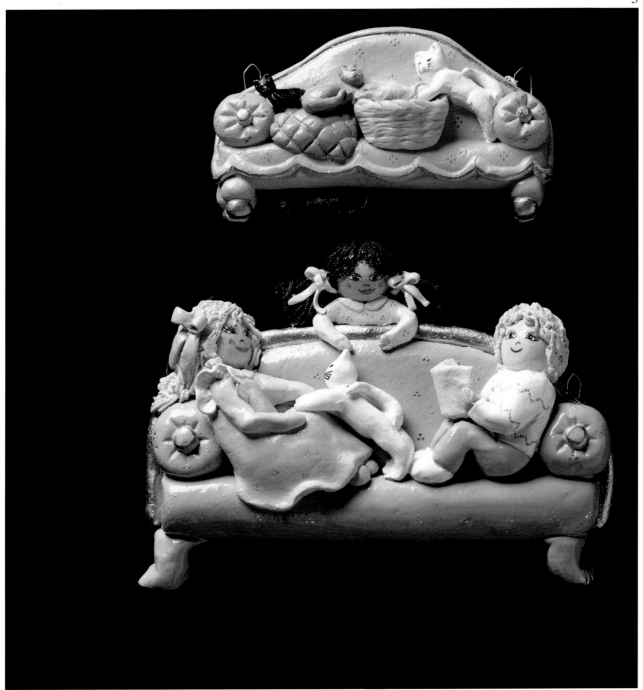

3. A great present for cat lovers. Make the top sofa as follows: first cut a curved piece of flat dough, and then fit the seat to that. Next come the legs, cushions and cats. The unpainted hollow basket has a twisted edge and pattern carved in. (K.W.)

The lilac-coloured sofa below has a thin roll round the flat dough. Just make the upper body and head of the girl behind the sofa. (K.W.)

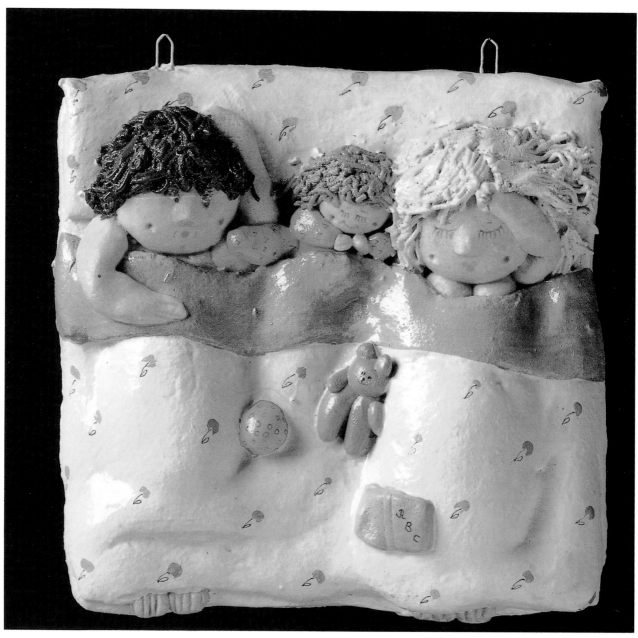

4

4. Mummy, Daddy and child in double bed. First roll out the dough for the bed, then pillows, figures and finally a cover. Use two pink-coloured paper-clips for hanging. (M.M.)

5. A picture of innocence: a
pair of twins stretching in bed.
To achieve a realistic effect
with the bedding, roll some
lace in the dough, making sure
that you obtain a clear imprint.
Then cut the points of the lace
with scissors. (B.P.)

6. A few moments of peace
with the newspaper. The
"mattress" is only $\frac{1}{2}$cm($\frac{1}{5}$in)
thick: on top, shape two
pillows, the man himself and
last of all the cover. (G.S)

1

2

1. A little Father Christmas with fine patterns on the cap and mittens. The doll on his arm has striped green clothes. (L.J.)

2. An attractive Advent calendar, consisting of several lumps of dough joined together to make a cloud. But you can also make it in one piece. Attach the angel-wings to this. Finally add the head, body and the balls for the hands and feet. The hair is squeezed out with the garlic press.

To hang the package, fasten paper-clips or loops of copper/brass wire. (K.L.)

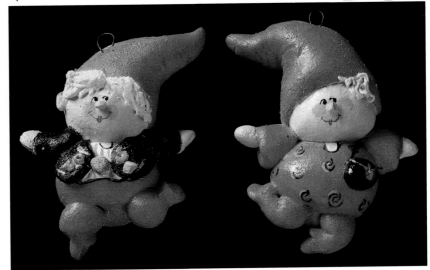

3. Why not make your own Christmas decorations? Roll out the dough to a thickness of about $\frac{1}{2}$cm($\frac{1}{5}$in), and take out the motifs using gingerbread shapes or cut them out with a spatula or table knife.

   You can make holes with a straw, or stick down a gold paper-clip or loop of wire in the top. You can paint patterns, after which sprinkle on glitter, that will adhere while the paint is drying.

5. Two simple figures with balls for hands and feet. As with the dresses, the aprons are cut out from thinly rolled dough, and wrinkled slightly under the bust. (K.L.)

4. A jolly pair of goblins: she has a little black bag, while he has a flower pattern on his jacket. (K.L.)

5

6. A simple dough-roll makes an ideal garland for candles: it should be slightly bigger than here, or the candles will be too close together. You can either buy brass-coated candleholders or make a hollow in the dough with the candle itself; decorate with petals of flattened balls and leaves.

The white candle-ring is from a thickly rolled piece of dough, and there are small yellow-painted dough-balls round the candleholder.

The green candle-ring has the five petals drawn to a point as a Star of Bethlehem.

7. A goblin boy and girl wearing scarves. Everything is made from dough coloured with powder and baked at a low temperature. The straw can be baked at the same time, or glued on afterwards. (B.J.)

7

8. The cats will also have milk on Christmas Eve. The apron is painted in a patchwork pattern. (K.L.)

9. This little candlestick (it will tolerate oven heat) has a garland made from dough at the bottom. Puncture the garland and glue dried flowers into the holes after baking. Attach the angel's hands to the garland and bake the candlestick and angel together at low temperature. Paint everything afterwards. (L.F.)

10. A snow-castle prior to being painted. Roll out a big piece of dough and bend it into a U-shape, then model the children and snowballs and fix on with a little water. Use two metal wires for hanging. Carve out the windows with a spatula or knife. (R.H.P.)

11. The snow-castle and children are now painted; only their faces and hands have retained their natural colour. (R.H.P.)

12. An old goblin in a cardigan; his long beard has been pressed through a garlic crusher. (K.L.)

10

12

11

13. Stars of Bethlehem as table decorations. Make the parts separately, then join them together to form the star. Place aluminium foil on the baking tray under the leaves so that they keep their curved shape. Make some extra leaves for scattering over the table cloth: they are excellent for covering stubborn stains. (J.L.)

14. A boy on skis made from a long U-shaped dough-roll. The ski-stick is a small piece of wood. It can fall (as in the picture) but be put back in the hand again. The strap on the ski-stick is of leather and the snow shoes of dough. The purl and plain stitched edges are carved with a spatula (or knife). (R.H.P.)

15. A decorative angel with dried flowers glued on after baking. The hair has been painted bronze and the wings gold. The shoes are also painted on. (L.F.)

16. A low-necked angel, singing her heart out. The wings are formed in one piece. The gold-painted hair is in plaits and a thin piece of brass wi acts as a hook for hanging. (I.J.)